IMAGES
of America

FORT DOUGLAS

IMAGES
of America

FORT DOUGLAS

Louwane Vansoolen and
the Fort Douglas Military Museum

ARCADIA
PUBLISHING

Published by Arcadia Publishing
Charleston, South Carolina

Printed in the United States of America

Library of Congress Control Number: 2009921911

For all general information contact Arcadia Publishing at:
Telephone 843-853-2070
Fax 843-853-0044
E-mail sales@arcadiapublishing.com
For customer service and orders:
Toll-Free 1-888-313-2665

Visit us on the Internet at www.arcadiapublishing.com

*This book is dedicated to all the veterans who have
passed through the gates of Fort Douglas.*

CONTENTS

ACKNOWLEDGMENTS

The photographs in this book have been collected from many sources, particularly from veterans who have been stationed at Fort Douglas or have spent time in the military. I wish to thank these patrons of the Fort Douglas Military Museum for their thoughtful gifts and stories. I want to thank the Utah State Historical Society, University of Utah's Marriott Library, and Daughters of the Utah Pioneers for letting me use some of the photographs from their collections. Ephriam Dickson III, museum curator, has been a great help. While visiting Washington, D.C., he took time to search the National Archives and returned with a great number of photographs that dealt with Fort Douglas from the beginning to the present. Also Robert Voyles, museum administrator, helped with some of the historical facts. Dr. Charles G. Hibbard, one of the museum's great volunteers, has been the most help in preparing the manuscript for this book. Dr. Hibbard has been on the Fort Douglas Museum Association Board for many, many years and has a vast knowledge of Fort Douglas and the military. His book *Fort Douglas, Utah: A Frontier Fort 1862–1991*, plus numerous articles and pamphlets he has written on the museum, has been at the core of my research into the events and timeline for this book. And finally thanks to all the staff, docents, and volunteers at the museum who have all added inspiration at different points while putting this book together.

INTRODUCTION

In the midst of the Civil War, Col. Patrick Edward Connor and the California-Nevada Volunteers were ordered to the Utah Territory for the purpose of guarding the Overland Mail Route; they arrived in October 1862. Concerned about secessionist activities in the area, Colonel Connor chose a location that allowed him to keep an eye on the Mormons. The post was originally called Camp Douglas, in honor of the recently deceased Illinois senator Stephen A. Douglas, who had been an ally of the West. The regiment established a garrison, gained military supremacy over the indigenous cultures, and began successful prospecting for mineral wealth in the surrounding mountains.

By the late 1860s, the mutual distrust between the army and the Mormons gave way to wary accommodation. The Mormons remained loyal to the Union, and the army's presence provided Salt Lake City with a much-needed infusion of money. By 1866, the California-Nevada Volunteers had all been discharged and replaced by army regulars from the 18th Infantry.

Camp Douglas became increasingly important in the western military establishment as a supply center for the fast-moving cavalry during the 1870s. As a result, in 1878, Camp Douglas became Fort Douglas. Toward the end of the century, the Indian Wars ended, but conflict with Spain increased. In 1901, Fort Douglas was upgraded to regimental headquarters, where troops were trained for service elsewhere.

During the two World Wars, the post served as a mobilization and training garrison, as well as a prisoner of war camp. In 1940, Fort Douglas was comprised of three separate bases: the fort, Salt Lake Airbase, and Wendover Bombing and Gunnery Range. In fact, the 7th Bomb Group, the unit that flew into Pearl Harbor the morning it was bombed, had been training at and left from Fort Douglas. During World War II, Fort Douglas served as the headquarters for the 9th Service Command and as a reception and separation center. In the years since World War II, Fort Douglas has served as headquarters for Reserve and National Guard units and as a support detachment for military activities in the area. The historic area of Fort Douglas was designated a National Historic Landmark in 1970. A tradition of granting and selling excess land and property to others in the area has existed throughout the history of the post. At one time, the post contained 10,525 acres; today the military occupies 58 acres. In 1874, Congress set aside 50 acres of the southwest corner of the post as a public cemetery, which became Mount Olivet Cemetery. In 1909, an additional 60 acres of the post were added to the cemetery. Congress also granted 60 acres to the University of Utah in 1894, an additional 32 acres in 1906, and another 61.5 acres in 1932.

In 1945, some 49 acres at the mouth of Emigration Canyon were granted to the Utah Pioneer Trails and Landmarks Association. In 1946, the Shriners bought several acres of land at the north boundary of the post to build their hospital. In 1947, the motor pool area located just west of the Annex Building was granted to the National Guard. In 1948, a total of 25 acres was transferred to the Veterans Administration for the construction of the Veterans Hospital on Foothill Boulevard. This same year, Salt Lake City obtained the triangular portion located between the university and the Veterans Hospital; the Bureau of Mines received 10 acres; several acres between Mount

Olivet Cemetery and Guardsman Way were transferred to the Utah National Guard; and the University of Utah acquired another 299 acres. In 1970, the several-thousand-acre Red Butte watershed was transferred to the U.S. Forest Service, and the University of Utah was granted the area now occupied by Research Park.

It was proposed that the post be closed in the 1860s, just prior to World War I, just after World War II, in 1967, in 1978, and again in 1988. The post survived all of these but the last. Consequently, federal legislation was passed in 1991 transferring approximately 51 acres, and any lands declared excess to the needs of the army in the future, to the University of Utah in exchange for state lands. In 1998, approximately 12 more acres were transferred to the university. The southern portion of Fort Douglas, including the historic buildings on Soldiers Circle, continues to be used as the headquarters of the Army Reserve Command and as a base of operation for U.S. Navy and Marine Reserves.

Fort Douglas has played an important role in Utah's economic, political, and social history. Its contributions to national defense have been equally distinctive. The post and its buildings have also contributed significantly to Utah's architectural heritage and have been an integral part of the University of Utah's history.

If one were to visit the fort today, he or she would still be able to see the original parade field that is covered with grass and lined with locust trees planted in the early 1900s. The University of Utah uses the field for soccer and lacrosse games and practice. Students from the university use the field in the winter for a good old-fashioned snowball fight. In the summer, the field is used for picnics or just to throw a football around. It is also a favorite spot to sit under a tree and study. Officer's Circle still stands with its Gothic sandstone buildings, now being used for student quarters rather than officers. The bandstand has been rebuilt on its original spot using the original drawings from the 1800s. The original post chapel still stands and is still being used for weddings. Many veterans who took their wedding vows during World War II have been back with their sweethearts to renew their vows. One can still see the Officers' Club that is being used for wedding receptions, meetings, and training sessions. Two of the old sandstone barracks still stand on the south side of the field and houses the Fort Douglas Military Museum. Salt Lake City has expanded through the years and now encircles the old fort, but the serenity and beauty of the 1900s can still be felt upon entering the area known as Fort Douglas.

HISTORY OF THE FORT DOUGLAS MILITARY MUSEUM

The Fort Douglas Military Museum was registered by the Center for Military History as an official museum of the U.S. Army Museum System on August 8, 1974, with the date of establishment being August 10, 1974. The commander of Fort Douglas had initiated the request on January 29, 1974.

In January 1975, the Fort Douglas Military Museum Association began its charter membership drive, and on June 18, 1975, the association was incorporated. Renovation of Building 32 also began in June of that year.

The museum was dedicated on October 26, 1975, and officially opened on May 14, 1976. The sponsoring headquarters was the 96th Army Reserve Command (ARCOM).

In 1981, Maj. Gen. Michael B. Kaufman initiated a fund-raising drive to develop Cannon Park and the statue of Maj. Gen. Patrick E. Connor. This project was completed in 1986.

The museum received certification from the Center of Military History on November 3, 1986. As a result of the fort turnover to the University of Utah in late 1988, the museum came under the sponsorship of the Utah National Guard, where it remains today.

In addition to Building 32, Buildings 31 and 55 were also identified as part of the museum complex. Both of these buildings are part of the current museum operations. In addition, Building 35, located to the south of the museum, has been under license from the U.S. Army Reserve since 2003.

In 2000, a complete review was made of the facilities and exhibits, and it was determined that a major renovation and expansion was needed. As a result, a $6-million plan was developed. As of this date of publication, an additional 6,000 square feet for a new main gallery and collection storage has been built and the existing electrical and HVAC systems have been replaced in the historical buildings.

—Col. Robert Voyles (Ret.)

One

COLONEL CONNOR AND THE ESTABLISHMENT OF CAMP DOUGLAS

Patrick Edward O'Connor established Camp Douglas and became its first commander. He was born on March 17, 1820, in Kerry County, Ireland. When he was very young, his parents immigrated to New York City, where he lived until on November 28, 1839, Patrick enlisted as a private in Company I, 1st Dragoons, which was the army's Native American fighting force. After completing his five-year enlistment, he was discharged and went into the mercantile business. In 1846, he immigrated to Texas and on May 6, 1846, mustered into Albert Sydney Johnston's command as a lieutenant and became a Texas foot rifleman in Texas's dispute with Mexico. At this time, he changed his name to Patrick E. Connor. After being honorably discharged, he moved to Stockton, California.

While in California, he was involved in many civic activities, married Johanna Connor, and achieved social and financial stature. In May 1853, he became a member of the California Rangers to help control outlaw disorder. In December 1856, a volunteer militia company, the Stockton Blues, was formed with Connor as first lieutenant; he later became captain of the group. Besides an interest in the military, Connor submitted design plans for the California State Capitol and later designed and built a new home in Stockton.

With the beginning of the Civil War in April 1861, Connor formed a 146-man company called the Union Guard. On August 23, Gov. John Downey issued a call for volunteer troops, and on September 4, Connor was mustered in as a colonel for the 3rd Infantry California Volunteers. Also during this time, Native American actions against the overland emigrant, mail, and telegraph lines increased in severity; on July 5, 1862, Connor's command was ordered to protect the Overland Mail Route. Connor was 42 years old when he assumed command of the Military District of Utah, which was comprised of the territories of Nevada and Utah.

On October 26, 1862, Colonel Connor established Camp Douglas in the foothills overlooking Salt Lake City, Utah. Besides the military, he was also interested in mining and was central to setting up four mining companies. He founded the town of Stockton, Utah, with the Pioneer Smelting Works in 1866. He was a very gifted soldier and was regarded as the best Indian fighter in the army. On March 13, 1865, Connor was promoted to brevet major general and was given command of the District of the Plains. Connor was mustered out of the military on April 30, 1866, after declining the offer of colonel in the regular army.

Retired Major General Connor is pictured in 1889. After military life, Connor kept busy with his mining business. He was president of the first Utah railroad system started by the Gentiles, owned and operated two steamboats on the Great Salt Lake, was appointed to command the Utah Territorial militia, became very active in the Liberal Party of Utah, and was involved in the installation of electricity for lighting in Salt Lake City. Patrick E. Connor died on December 17, 1891, and is buried in the Post Cemetery at Fort Douglas. (Utah State Historical Society Photograph Collection.)

The 3rd California Infantry Band is shown here in 1862. With the beginning of the Civil War in April 1861, President Lincoln was anxious to keep the California mail route open and protected and issued a call for volunteers. In July 1862, Connor's command was ordered to protect the Overland Mail Route between central Nevada and South Pass, Wyoming. The 3rd and 2nd California Volunteers leaving Camp McDougal for Utah consisted of about 1,000 infantry and 500 cavalry men; a battery of field artillery; 200 wagons, each capable of carrying 3,000 pounds of supplies; three wagon ambulances; and several carriages of officers' families.

This cavalry quartermaster sergeant is wearing a dress uniform typically worn during the 1860s. His black felt hat is called a "hardee." Non-commissioned officers wore a single-breasted dark-blue jacket with gold buttons and brass shoulder scales. Trousers were light-blue wool with a stripe up the outside seam. The cavalry members were issued a carbine, a pistol, and a cavalry saber. The nature of Native American warfare gave little opportunity to use the saber, and they were routinely left on post as useless encumbrances more suited for guard duty or parades. Rifles used by the California Volunteers were mostly Sharps Model 1859 (a percussion, breech-loading, .52-caliber) or the Model 1841 or "Mississippi" rifle. The revolver most used was a Colt revolver Model 1851 "Navy," a six-shot, .36-caliber gun.

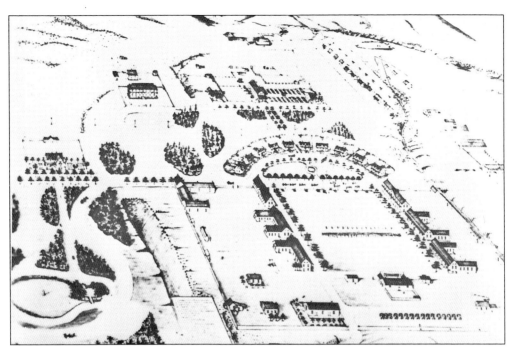

Upon arrival in the Salt Lake Valley, Connor and his California Volunteers selected a campsite on a bench overlooking the Salt Lake Valley. Four days later, Colonel Connor issued Order No. 14 on October 26, 1862, officially founding Camp Douglas. The reservation as laid out by the commanding officer included 2,560 acres. In later years, as the fort grew, it would consist of 10,525 acres. This 1888 drawing shows an overview of what Camp Douglas will look like. The canyon above the fort is Red Butte Canyon; not only did this canyon supply water but also sandstone used in the construction of most of the buildings on post.

Colonel Connor named Camp Douglas after the Honorable Stephen L. Douglas, made famous by his debates with Abraham Lincoln. He defeated Lincoln in the race for the Senate but later lost the presidency. Douglas was the outstanding champion of the West while a U.S. senator, one of the reasons Camp Douglas was named after him. Camp Douglas became an important location for the military in the West and was later renamed Fort Douglas after it was rebuilt in 1875–1876 by Col. John E. Smith, commander of the 14th Infantry.

Alexander Badger, a civilian employed as a clerk at the post, enclosed this drawing in a letter to his mother in 1863. With winter approaching fast, the soldiers immediately set out to build shelters to protect them from the harsh Utah weather. The buildings constructed were mere dugouts: there were 32 pits, each 13 feet square and 4 feet deep, over which canvas tents were erected. They each housed 12 men. Connor described them as being dry and well ventilated. The soldiers called them Connor tents. (Missouri Historical Society.)

The troops were barely settled in for the winter when in January 1863 Connor mobilized 300 men for a march to what is now southern Idaho to aid settlers and trappers who were the target of raiding Native Americans. In bitter cold and deep snow, Connor's men set out. At least 70 men became casualties of frozen feet while en route. Bear Hunter's Shoshoni Indians were encamped in a narrow ravine that drained into the Bear River; thus it is known as the Battle (Massacre) at Bear River. Most of the Native Americans remained in the ravine and fought it out to the last. This would be the last major fight with Native Americans in the territory.

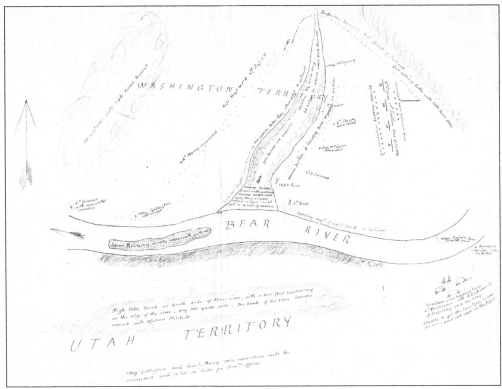

This map of the Battle of Bear River was drawn by James H. Martineau. James was an eyewitness to the battle and was able to draw the layout right after the battle. (Church of Jesus Christ of Latter-day Saints Church Archives.)

By February 1864, Colonel Connor's quarters and office had been constructed, and he moved his family—wife, Johanna, and son Maurice—from Salt Lake City to the post. (National Archives.)

Connor's daughter Katherine Frances ("Kate") was one of the first children born at Camp Douglas. Patrick Edward ("Ned") was born in Salt Lake City in 1866. Connor named the first Gentile railroad engine after his daughter, the "Kate Connor," and a steamboat owned by Connor was also named the *Kate Connor*, the first vessel on the Great Salt Lake. (Utah State Historical Society Photograph Collection.)

Colonel Connor brought mining to Utah and encouraged miners and rich friends to start developing the mining industry in Utah. He permitted his troops to explore on their off-duty time, and a number of mines were discovered. Brigham Young had opposed the development of mining by his people because he did not believe the plan was economically sound, but he urged his followers to work for the miners, using their earned cash to develop and expand their agricultural enterprises. Connor hastened to write mining laws and organize a mining district, which was called West Mountain Mining District. Because of his involvement in mining, Connor became known as the "Father of Mining in Utah."

Two

THE EARLY YEARS

Most frontier forts were located in regions of the West that were inhabited only by hostile Native Americans. This must have made for a very monotonous and dull life for the soldier who had nothing better to do than perform his rigid, organized routine each day. Even though Camp Douglas was located just a few miles from a rather large community, they were Mormons, and the distrust between the military and the prominent religion must have been very uncomfortable and kept the soldiers at a distance.

The routine for a soldier in the 19th century included three roll calls each day, the daily mounting of the guard, the necessary fatigues, drills, and an evening dress parade at retreat. Between these duties, the men spent their time lounging around the barracks and doing whatever they pleased, but they had to always remain within the sound of the bugle.

Fatigue duty was the same as manual labor: constructing roads, building living quarters and other structures, installing telegraph lines, and many more jobs that were essential to keeping a frontier fort operating. Most soldiers felt they were being exploited as cheap labor and grumbled about such duties even though they were given an extra 20¢ for their labor. Men who were experienced in carpentry or stonemasonry were given extra duty pay of 35¢. Less strenuous fatigue duty included kitchen detail, stable policing, orderly, and a host of other daily necessities.

Payday was an important day in camp, but a soldier soon learned his pay did not go very far. Some of it went to pay off debts that he may have with the company barber, laundress, cobbler, or tailor. Also he may have credit with the "sutler store" to pay off. Some soldiers sent money home or set up a savings with the paymaster that was withdrawn on his discharge. Other activities such as gambling and drinking took a large piece of their pay, and often civilians would be waiting at the gate on payday to help the soldier spend his money on liquor and extra food.

This is a view of Camp Douglas looking southwest with Salt Lake just out of view in the background. In just a few short years (1862 to 1864), approximately 85 adobe and wood structures were erected on the Camp Douglas reservation. These structures were very simple in design and were put up quickly as the California Volunteers thought Camp Douglas would be a temporary military post. (National Archives.)

The Mormons and the military had great distrust for each other. The Mormons felt that the military was going to imprison their leader, Brigham Young. It was rumored that a telescope was set up atop the Mormon leader's house, and through it the Mormons watched activities at Camp Douglas. Connor felt the Mormons were full of treason and needed to be watched every minute. One night, cannons boomed and the Mormons hastily mobilized an emergency force of militia to surround the residence of their leader, but no conflict ensued. It was later discovered that the 11-gun salute was fired to celebrate the news that Connor had been brevetted a brigadier general for his outstanding victory over the Native Americans at Bear River.

The Company Quarters (barracks) for the enlisted men at Camp Douglas were located on the south side of the parade field. These long buildings were made of wood and whitewashed. Each building consisted of cots lining the interior on two sides of the room for the men of that particular company. A fireplace was placed at each end of the building to supply heat during the winter. Comfort and privacy were unknown conveniences for the early soldiers of the Old West. (National Archives.)

This is a view of Camp Douglas on the north side of the parade field in 1864. The building on the left is a sutler store with Company Quarters lined up behind it. Sutler stores showed up at most army forts and camps and were run by civilian peddlers to provision the troops. Some stores had well-stocked shelves that included canned foods, cigars, sugar, flour, tea, coffee, liquor, salt, sardines, medicines, and notions. In most forts, there was no competition and prices were very high for the goods that were sold. Both military and civilian wagon trains on their way west purchased goods at the sutler store. (National Archives.)

The guardhouse, located on the west side of the parade field, was one of the first buildings made of stone. This building consisted of a prisoner's room (11 by 14 feet), three cells, guard room (14 by 23 feet), a tool room, and an office of the guard room (9 by 10 feet). Discipline varied from one company to another depending on the company commander over that unit. Fear of punishment was the basis of discipline. Soldiers were expected to live by the Army Regulations and the Articles of War, more often known as the "thou-shalt-nots." (National Archives.)

Building 79 is the ordnance building, used to store ammunition and arms. This building was located just north of the guardhouse on the west side of the parade field and made of stone with no windows, just a large locked door and a shingled roof. (National Archives.)

Each company was authorized four laundresses, who were usually wives of enlisted men on post and were housed in these small cabins. A laundress not only did the men's laundry but also took on the role of nurse, midwife, and babysitter. She might make as much as $30 a month (much more than an enlisted soldier for that time) washing uniforms. This row of cabins located along Red Butte Creek was more often known as "Suds Row." Besides housing, laundresses often received a ration of food, fuel, and medical supplies for their services. (National Archives.)

This 1864 view shows Camp Douglas, Post Headquarters, and Officers' Quarters located on the east side of the parade field. Most forts at this time were located in dry, deserted areas of the frontier. If a man was lucky enough to be sent to Camp Douglas with its mountain range, streams, and good game, he was considered very fortunate. (National Archives.)

The 12-pound Howitzer was part of the California Volunteers' heavy armament along with caisson and limber. Under General Connor's command, they took part in the Powder River Campaign of 1865. Three columns were to converge on the hostile Sioux, Cheyenne, and Arapaho in Wyoming, but they were not well organized, had insufficient supplies, and had poor guides and maps. Only General Connor's column achieved any success when he surprised an Arapaho Indian village and captured it. He burned the village and captured most of the horse herd. (National Archives.)

Capt. Charles Hempstead was superintendant of the U.S. Mint in San Francisco before he enlisted in the army. In 1863, Colonel Connor assigned him to be the editor of Camp Douglas's first newspaper, the *Union Vedette*. He became the post's first provost marshal of Salt Lake City and established his headquarters in a building opposite the Tabernacle on South Temple Street. Charles Hempstead was well liked by the Mormons, and after his discharge from the military, he became the U.S. Attorney for the district of Utah in February 1866.

This was the print office of the *Union Vedette* in 1866. The *Deseret News* was the Mormon-owned newspaper at the time and quite often complained of the military's presence, so Connor established the *Union Vedette*, with the first publication on November 26, 1863. It was a post newspaper, and its tone was strongly anti-Mormon. The paper was published weekly until January 1864, when it became a daily newspaper. (National Archives.)

This is the *Daily Union Vedette Newspaper* from February 26, 1866. Its motto was "A champion, brave, alert and strong; to aid the right, oppose the wrong." The name "Vedette" means a mounted sentinel in advance of the main group, to warn of approaching danger. The *Vedette* had a wide circulation in Utah and neighboring states and was the first "Gentile" newspaper in Utah. The last issue was published November 27, 1867. (Utah State Historical Society Photograph Collection.)

This view is of the surgeon's quarters, Building 55. Dr. Edward Perry Vollum was the surgeon from 1870 to 1876 and had a street named after him. While stationed at Fort Douglas, he wrote a complete medical history of the post. This building is made of logs and adobe with 18-inch-thick walls and was constructed in 1863. Today this is the only structure still standing from that era. (National Archives.)

This is the first hospital built at Camp Douglas, pictured in 1866. The building was made of logs and whitewashed to give it a clean look. After the construction of a new hospital in 1875, this old hospital was remodeled and used for recreation and as a meeting place. (National Archives.)

This photograph was taken in 1866 and shows the post commander's quarters. Colonel Connor and his family may have used this building until newer quarters were constructed. The residence next to this structure housed six officers. (National Archives.)

The officers' quarters of Building 43 is divided down the center with the living quarters mirroring each other on both sides of the wall. The building was made of logs and had been whitewashed. Most officers' quarters at this time had a parlor or sitting room in the front portion of the structure with bedrooms toward the back and a kitchen in the very back of the building (the part that looks like an add-on). (National Archives.)

These log non-commissioned officers' quarters, in 1866, did not offer much in the way of comfort, but they did give the officers a bit more privacy than what they would have if they were housed in a barracks with sometimes up to 50 enlisted men. (National Archives.)

The flagpole was placed at the east end of the parade field in 1862 and is still located in that same spot today. The building directly in back of the flagpole is post headquarters, Building 45. Flagpoles in frontier forts at this time took on the look of a ship's mast. It might be some kind of tradition, or maybe they just did not have straight poles tall enough to reach the height needed and had to splice two poles together. In Utah, there are no tall straight pines. (National Archives.)

Camp Douglas Headquarters, Building 45, located at the east end of the parade field, was centrally located to the fort's activities. The post commander's office was probably located here. Headquarters was an important part of daily activity in the military, giving direction to every aspect of army life. (National Archives.)

This is a photograph of the bakery, one of the first structures on the post made of stone. The bakery was contracted by a civilian company run by Elias Morris. Morris was born in Wales and learned the mason trade from his father. In 1853, he was put in charge of building an iron works and blast furnace in Cedar City, Utah. He worked on the Salt Lake temple foundation in 1860. In 1864, his company worked on most of the buildings along Main Street in Salt Lake City. His masons were paid very well and received $25 to $30 per day. (National Archives.)

This photograph shows the stables and teamster shops in 1866. This was a very important part of a frontier fort. Horses, mules, and wagons kept the army mobile. Plus all supplies and travel were done with wagons, horses, and mules. The importance of taking good care of their animals and equipment was crucial to the survival of the fort. (National Archives.)

This was the wheelwright's shop in 1866. The wheelwright built and repaired the old wooden wagon wheels and sometimes made barrels for use on the post. Wagons, caissons, and limbers often needed repair work, and the wheelwright, along with the blacksmith, was called upon to do this important work. (National Archives.)

Col. Phillip de Trobriand was commander of the 13th Infantry. The army became involved in the government's crusade against polygamy, which was being practiced by the Mormons at that time. Colonel de Trobriand was not sympathetic to the anti-polygamy efforts of the local officials. He was transferred and succeeded by Col. Henry Morrow, who was thought to be more compliant with government wishes. A street at Fort Douglas is named for Colonel de Trobriand.

Three

FORT EXPANSION
AND MOBILIZATION

An extensive construction program was begun at Camp Douglas in the mid-1870s. Before this renewal of the camp, living conditions were far from ideal. Soldiers had to cope with improperly heated and poorly constructed barracks. Disease and vermin were rampant, and many soldiers were ill. Sanitation was a big problem; food was not handled well and most of the time not cooked properly.

The Surgeon's Report in 1872 stated, "Of the 364 men at the Camp, fully 216 suffered from typhoid fever or some similar disease; 230 had diarrhea or dysentery; 54 suffered from rheumatism; and 101 had contracted bronchitis." This is on a post that is within just a few miles of the largest city in Utah.

Clearly Camp Douglas needed to be restructured and rebuilt to provide the soldiers with better living conditions. Up to this time, the adobe and wood structures at Camp Douglas were put up for temporary use only. In 1875, the government decided to make Camp Douglas a permanent army post. Construction of better-designed and permanent buildings of barracks, offices, living quarters, and shops was begun, improving the conditions for the army in Utah. The new buildings were erected using sandstone quarried at the mouth of Red Butte Canyon.

Camp Douglas was renamed Fort Douglas after it was rebuilt in 1875–1876 and made a permanent military post by Col. John E. Smith, commanding the 14th Infantry. At this time, the regular army took over the fort and the volunteer units were released or moved to other areas.

The fort was considerably enlarged during the new building program from 1904 to 1911, when the new red-brick barracks around Soldier Circle were built—Buildings 91, 92, 93, 94, 96, and 97—to house 176 men each, and the band barracks, Building 98, for 33 men. Other buildings completed included a bakery, guardhouse, bachelor officers' quarters, bowling alley, Post Exchange, warehouses, and post hospital. These buildings departed from the building designs of previous projects.

The tremendous building program of the first decade in the new century was culminated in 1910 with the installation of electric lights in all quarters and administrative buildings. The following year, steam heating was installed in living quarters.

Sandstone buildings were erected starting in 1874. This photograph shows one of the classic Gothic-style homes that started going up all over Fort Douglas. At this time, in 1885, Col. Gehil A. McCook, the commander of the 6th Infantry, and his family were living here. The people standing on the porch are Kathleen McCook, daughter Lucy and Colonel McCook.

Twelve-pound Howitzers are shown on the parade field with soldiers in fatigue uniforms on review. The building on the right is one of the newly erected barracks.

U.S. president Rutherford B. Hayes, the man standing at the top of the stairs, visited Fort Douglas in 1879. Retired general Patrick Connor is seated on the right at the top of the stairs. President Hayes was the first of many U.S. presidents to visit Fort Douglas.

This stereoscopic photograph was taken about 1879 and is one of many stereoscopic images taken of the fort and its surroundings during this time. The man sitting at the top of the stairs is Bvt. Brig. Gen. John E. Smith with his wife and mother seated on each side. Colonel Smith was commander of the 14th Infantry in 1874.

Soldiers stand at attention on the parade field facing west with the band out front. The new sandstone houses in the background make up what is known as Officer's Circle. These Gothic Revival–style buildings are still standing today and are used by the University of Utah. Readers can also see the bandstand in the center directly behind the flagpole.

The transcontinental railroad was completed in May 1869, which meant that troops from Camp Douglas could be quickly transported to the scene of conflict in a matter of days instead of weeks. In the next 15 years, companies from the fort would do just that. The twin defeats of Custer and Crook in 1876 resulted in a call for reinforcements, and in late June, four companies of the 14th Infantry boarded a train for Wyoming to join Gen. George Crook's command. General Crook followed a trail for over two months and in September surprised a village of Sioux Indians under Chief American Horse near Slim Buttes, Dakota Territory, and captured the village. (Daughters of Utah Pioneers.)

The 3rd California Infantry Band was mustered out en route to Utah, and upon arrival in Salt Lake, a camp band was organized under principal musician James Condell. A wooden Victorian Gothic bandstand was erected in 1876 and located at the east end of the parade field, just below Officer's Circle and overlooking Salt Lake Valley. Some of the U.S. Army's most renowned bands performed here, including the 24th Infantry (Buffalo Soldiers), who arrived at the post in 1896.

Part of military life consists of pomp and ceremony. The three soldiers in this photograph are the color guard presenting the colors in dress uniforms. The same color guard ceremony goes on today much the same as in the 1800s. About the only changes are the uniforms and the number of stars on the U.S. flag.

The new guardhouse is considerably larger than the earlier guardhouse, making this building much more comfortable for the guards, and sanitary conditions were better with less crowded cells and rooms for those occupying this building. (National Archives.)

Shown are the commanding officer's quarters at Camp Douglas in 1881. The residing officer at this time was probably Col. A. McCook, commander of the 6th Infantry. The 6th U.S. Volunteers were called "Galvanized Yankees." They were Confederate soldiers who volunteered to serve as Indian fighters rather than go to a prisoner-of-war camp.

This photograph is looking south from one of the officer's residences. The building on the right is the post administration office, which later became the Officer's Club, and next to that is one of the barracks on the north side of the parade field. The houses on the left are officers' quarters on Officer's Circle.

With the addition of new family living quarters constructed at the fort, more wives and children of officers started making Fort Douglas their home. As can be seen in this photograph, a woman's touch is present in this officer's yard with a fountain, urns, lawn furniture, and a statue. Fort life would start taking on a more civilized and cultured appearance with the ladies making their way into military life.

The original bandstand was destroyed by fire, and a new one was built on the same spot in 1912. The new bandstand was a much less ornamental structure than the Gothic Revival look of the original bandstand.

Officers' quarters in 1883 were made of adobe and whitewashed. At this time, Lieutenant Taggart is in residence here. In 1883, the 6th Infantry with Companies A through I and K are at the fort. There are 35 officers and 516 enlisted men.

Before the post chapel was built, services were held in the chapel tent, a gift of the Presbyterian Church of San Francisco. The first services were conducted in 1862, with the Reverend John Anderson of San Francisco as chaplain. He presided at the first burials in the new cemetery after the Bear River Battle. The first building used as a chapel was west of the parade ground and was a combination recreation hall, schoolroom, concert hall, and chapel.

In the fall of 1883, ground was broken for the chapel on the north side of the post at a cost of $4,500. Not until June 1910 was it equipped with electric lights. An $800 fire occurred in January 1922, but the damage was repaired. The writing on the wall in this interior photograph of the chapel reads, "Righteousness Exalteth a Nation: But Sin is a Reproach to Any People."

In 1874, the 14th Infantry arrived under the command of Col. John Smith, and that year, Gen. Philip Sheridan visited the post and noted, "I have seen no other post in the service where the quarters are so utterly worthless as those at Camp Douglas." The previous year, construction had begun on a new two-story barracks, and in the fall of 1874, an ambitious construction program began. This photograph was taken in 1884 of a line of wood and stone barracks. (National Archives.)

Each barracks had two to three potbellied stoves for heat, with kerosene lamps hung from the ceiling for light, a rack for the rifles, and maybe a table with a few chairs, plus the all-important spittoon. Each enlisted soldier could expect to receive two blankets, sheets, a pillow, a footlocker for personal items, and a shelf hung with a curtain for hanging uniforms. (National Archives.)

These barracks are located on the south side of the parade field. The first two barracks are made of wood, but the last three are made of sandstone with the far one being a two-story building. The buildings are numbered, from left to right, 33, 32, 31, 30, and 29. Buildings 31 and 32 are still in use today as part of the Fort Douglas Military Museum. Building 33 burned down with only part of the sandstone foundation remaining to mark the spot. (National Archives.)

This is the administration building or post headquarters, Building 49. This building eventually became the Officer's Club. The University of Utah owns this lovely building now, and in 2001 they restored it to its original glory. They also added a new wing in the back plus parking. Today it is used as a meeting and reception hall. (National Archives.)

The officers of the 16th and 21st Infantries, Light, and Battery D in 1888 are, from left to right, starting (back row) Captain Ward, Lt. Sam Allen, Lt. G. Putnam, Lt. Maury Nickols, Capt. S. Jocelyn, Lt. H. Styer, Lt. W. Johnston; (middle row) Captain Allen, Col. Brevet Hale, Captain Morrison, Captain Palmer, Dr. Meacham, Colonel Blunt, Captain Kinzie, Lieutenant Massy; (front row) Captain Lassiter, Lieutenant Young, Lieutenant Gregg, Captain Richards, and Captain Dunning. (Army War College Archives.)

Here is an inspection on the parade field in the 1890s. With the Native American uprisings having ended, the fort saw only routine activity until the war with Spain in 1898. Through the efforts of Utah's U.S. senator, Thomas Kearns, Camp Douglas became a regimental post on December 30, 1878, ensuring its survival during the 1890s when many frontier posts were closed.

The 6th Infantry replaced the 14th Infantry in 1881, and a decade of peace greeted the newcomers. New construction in the 1880s and 1890s included four new wooden barracks built to house artillery troops that had arrived, a stone stable capable of housing 98 horses or mules, and housing for four sergeants, the first quarters specifically designated for enlisted personnel. (National Archives.)

Fort Douglas Boulevard looks south with the headquarters building on the right. Contracted supplies of food, clothing, and fuel for the troops in the 1800s cost the government $150,000 a year. The profit to a contractor for these goods was approximately $50,000 of the total. Most of the contractors at this time were Mormons from the Salt Lake area, which must have greatly helped the local economy. The first demonstration telephone in Utah was installed at Fort Douglas in 1879. The other end of the line was in Salt Lake City.

Buildings 61, 62, and 63 on Connor Road were built in 1891. These structures were better known as NCO (non-commissioned officer) Quarters. (National Archives.)

The cemetery is pictured in 1897 on Memorial Day. The post cemetery was laid out in December 1862, when the first death occurred in the command. A collection of $1,631.50 was raised to build a monument to those who fell at Bear River, and there were sufficient funds to pay for planting locust trees and to build a wall and gate. The memorial was dedicated on the first anniversary of the Battle of Bear River, with Capt. Charles H. Hempstead giving the dedication address.

Gen. Patrick Connor was buried in the post cemetery. The plaque reads, "Patrick Edward Connor, Brigadier General and Brevet Major General U.S. Volunteers, Born March 17, 1820. Died December 17, 1891. Camped in this vicinity with his California volunteers October 20, 1862. Established Camp Douglas, Utah October 26, 1862. Participated in the Battles of Buena Vista, Bear River and Tongue River. The Father of Utah Mining. Erected 1930 by the Garrison of Fort Douglas, Utah, Assisted by the Utah Historical Landmarks Association and Patriotic Citizens of the West."

Each tombstone has its own story. The inscription on this stone reads, "In Memory of Dr. J. King Robinson who was assassinated Oct. 22, 1866, Aged 50 years, 5 Mo. & 10 Days, 'Vengeance is mine: I will repay, saith the Lord.'" Dr. Robinson was a surgeon who arrived here with Colonel Connor's army in 1862. On the night of October 22, 1866, he was called out. Within blocks of his house, he was clubbed and shot to death simply because he had filed a claim of ownership on what was later known as Wasatch Springs. It was believed Porter Rockwell killed him.

9th Cavalry Trooper 1891
Privates James Satchell & Samuel Tipton

Privates James Satchell and Samuel Tipton were part of the 9th Cavalry. October 1896 marked the arrival of Utah's first African American regiment, the U.S. Army 24th Infantry. At this time, there were only four African American units in the U.S. Army; they were composed of white officers and black enlisted men.

The 24th Infantry Regimental Band was well liked and in great demand while stationed at Fort Douglas. Being an excellent band, it played for social events throughout the Salt Lake Valley. On Sunday evenings and on holidays, they entertained the citizens of Salt Lake and fellow soldiers at the post bandstand.

The mostly white communities of Salt Lake Valley were not happy about having the 24th Infantry stationed at Fort Douglas. U.S. senator Frank Cannon even met with the Secretary of War about the regiment but was unable to have the unit transferred elsewhere. It was not long before the 24th Infantry soldiers and their families proved to be well-educated, sociable, and strong patriotic citizens and were soon welcomed into the community.

In 1898, the 24th Infantry was among the first troops to leave for Cuba during the Spanish-American War. There they performed valiantly, making the charge up San Juan Hill and suffering heavy casualties. After the war, they volunteered to remain and nurse the sick. They had 167 cases of fever resulting in 23 deaths.

Marching on the streets of Salt Lake City, the 24th Infantry takes part in the Pioneer Jubilee Parade on July 24, 1897. As the 24th Infantry left on the train for deployment to Cuba, many Salt Lake and Provo citizens, both black and white, turned out to bid them farewell. Their bravery and patriotism of country and duty in war brought honor to them and their unit. A large turnout of citizens joyfully welcomed them back at the end of their campaign.

The African American soldiers of the 24th Infantry from Fort Douglas are marching down Main Street in Salt Lake City around 1898. The troops may possibly be returning from Cuba at the end of the Spanish-American War. After Cuba, the regiment returned to Fort Douglas and in 1900 departed for the Philippines and another dirty, bloody conflict.

The U.S. Army bivouacked at Fort Douglas. The location of this photograph is where the University of Utah's Medical Center now stands. In 1902, the war in the Philippines was over and the 12th Infantry was transferred to Fort Douglas and Fort Duchesne. (National Archives.)

This photograph was taken in 1894 of Company I, 16th Infantry, U.S. Army, made up of Brule Sioux Indians. The company arrived at Fort Douglas about 1893 but was gone after only two years because of the high rate of illness in the company.

This is the interior of one of the barracks that housed the 16th Infantry, Company I. The Brule Sioux Indians who made up this company were from the Rosebud Indian Station. The Brule are part of the Great Sioux Nation that was at one time located in the Black Hills area. The white man found gold, and they were all moved to a reservation. (National Archives.)

Maj. John Milton Thompson commanded the 24th Infantry from 1898 to 1899. By 1901, he was the colonel of the 23rd Infantry and served with his regiment in the Philippines during the Philippine Insurrection. When his regiment returned home, they came by way of the Suez Canal and the Straits of Gibraltar, becoming the first U.S. Army regiment to circumnavigate the globe.

The group of men, women, and children in this photograph are attending some kind of formal military event. The women on post, especially officers' wives, were keen to create recreational and social events for the participation of the families. They often invented reasons for getting together such as sewing bees, luncheons, riding, hunting, and fishing. These events were often scheduled on a weekly basis and participated in by all.

Each summer, the field artillery units would conduct training exercises in the Strawberry Valley. Strawberry Valley now holds the Strawberry Reservoir and is located about 80 miles southeast of Fort Douglas. Digs are conducted about every summer in the Strawberry Valley for artifacts left by the army and the state militia while on training maneuvers in the area.

On July 15, 1908, a large joint exercise with the army and state militia was coming together. Their destination was Fort Russell, Wyoming, by way of the Denver and Rio Grande Railroad. The troops were marched from Fort Douglas to the Rio Grande depot on the west side of Salt Lake. The column consisted of the general staff followed by the band, six infantry companies, a machine-gun platoon, a hospital detachment, and a wagon train—a total of 24 officers and 453 enlisted men.

Up until Custer's Last Stand, most soldiers in the army were not very good marksmen with rifle or pistol. The government felt that the price of ammunition was too high to have regular target practice. After Little Big Horn, Congress was forced to provide money to promote good marksmanship. Soon after, soldiers started competing with other units throughout the United States for the honor of being the best shot in the country. The first target range at Fort Douglas was located just north of the post, where the University Hospital is now located.

This photograph was taken in front of one of the barracks on the north side of the parade field. Posing in the photograph are men from the 18th Infantry, Company K, U.S. Army, on October 31, 1901. The 18th Infantry arrived at Fort Douglas on October 20, 1901, and was commanded by Maj. George S. Young. The regiment consisted of 355 enlisted men and 20 officers and staff.

The Post Exchange (PX) is shown in this photograph around 1906. The first PX at Fort Douglas was set up in part of one of the barracks and opened in 1889. Up until this time, soldiers would purchase items the government did not issue them from the Post Trader or sutler store, where they were charged outrageous prices.

U.S. Army officers pose in front of one of the Gothic Revival buildings in 1902. In 1894, the University of Utah was granted land for a new campus by Congress of 60 acres; in 1906, they were given another 32 acres of federal land. Some of the old buildings erected at this time are still in use today on a horseshoe-shaped road east of the parade field. Also about this time, roads were being constructed to connect the fort with city streets. Congress passed a bill that authorized a road through the fort to Emigration Canyon, now known as Wasatch Drive.

These are stables with a picket line of horses and mules. The two soldiers in the photograph are Gabe May and Pvt. Lorie James Bartlow of the 22nd Battery, Light Field Artillery, around 1905. Horses were still a big part of the military at this time for movement of supplies and men.

A cavalry recruitment poster asks local civilians from Utah to sign up "and have a courageous friend," the horse being man's noblest companion.

THE HORSE IS MAN'S NOBLEST COMPANION

JOIN THE
CAVALRY
and have a courageous friend
U.S. ARMY RECRUITING OFFICE:

The caption on this photograph reads, "Fort Douglas Machine Gun Co. 1906." Soldiers are lined up with mules on the parade field in front of the barracks.

This photograph was taken July 12, 1908. By the 1900s, Fort Douglas was experiencing many families settling into quarters on post. At this time in history, all the fighting and military campaigns were being fought in foreign lands, leaving the frontier posts quiet and peaceful. The government had started to open schools on post. Not only the children of the soldiers were being schooled, but local children in the vicinity of the fort were allowed into the schools. In some cases, the soldiers themselves were taught reading, writing, and math.

Building 512, the Fort Douglas Hospital, was constructed in 1909. Up until this time, the small hospital in use did provide medical attention to the soldiers but was usually crowded—with ill together with the not so ill and in some cases with contagious patients.

While on a visit to Salt Lake City, Pres. William Howard Taft views the troops at Fort Douglas on September 25, 1909. After a banquet in his honor, President Taft told Colonel Scott, "This is the first review I have seen since I became President and it is the finest I have ever seen." Also in this photograph is Gov. William Spry, the governor of Utah.

Construction of Officer's Circle was begun in 1874. Capt. W. Davis, acting quartermaster, supervised the construction, and the soldiers provided the labor. The red sandstone in these buildings was quarried just south of the mouth of Red Butte Canyon and hauled down a steep road to the post. A few civilian masons and carpenters supervised the troops in building the beautiful Gothic-style buildings, which still enchant all who visit the post today.

Shoveling snow-packed roads on post is just one of many routine activities for soldiers during the winter months. These soldiers are working on what is now called Potter Street just in front of the line of barracks on the south side of the parade field.

The U.S. Army's 15th Infantry was on maneuvers in Colorado in 1910. This tent probably served as headquarters for the regiment. The 15th Infantry arrived at Fort Douglas on January 13, 1907, with Companies A through I, K, L, and M consisting of 731 enlisted men and 48 officers. Col. Walter S. Scott was the commander.

The Post Exchange was set up for the 15th Infantry while on maneuvers between Wyoming and Colorado during the summer of 1910. The 15th had performed courageously in both the Boxer Rebellion in China and the Philippine Insurrection.

The 15th Infantry hikes into Palmer Lake on maneuvers in 1910. This was an annual event for the men at Fort Douglas. This Camp of Instruction took them from Cheyenne, Wyoming, to Denver, Colorado.

This encampment site was set up at Camp Otis, Wyoming. The 15th Infantry Band is taking advantage of a beautiful day to practice while on maneuvers.

The 15th Infantry Band is loading an escort wagon with all its instruments, stands, music, field equipment, and tents in the summer of 1910 at Fort Collins, Colorado.

Twenty-five officers, 649 enlisted men, 45 horses, and 92 mules left on the Union Pacific Railroad for Cheyenne, Wyoming. These men are pitching their tents at Camp Otis, Wyoming. The soldiers at this Camp of Instruction followed the old Overland and Cherokee Trails.

An ambulance of the 15th Infantry is pulled by four mules in 1910 at Fort Collins, Colorado. At this time in history, most of the summer encampments were attended by both the regular army and the National Guard.

The army kept in touch with the higher echelons by telegraph. This is the 15th Infantry's telegraph station at Camp Otis, Wyoming, in 1910.

The army travels on its stomach—so they say—and this is what a mess call in the field looks like. The caption on this photograph reads, "Co. F at Chow, Virginiadale, Colorado, 1910."

A soldier and his faithful horse from the 15th Infantry are training while on maneuvers in Colorado. The caption reads, "A Scout Attacked by the Enemy."

A streetcar line ran up to Fort Douglas Boulevard through a narrow ravine, now known as Chapel Glen, between the chapel and post headquarters. Following terrain of a gentler slope, the Salt Lake City and Fort Douglas Railway line ran along the north side of Red Butte Creek. An artillery parade ground, near Building 105, was known as "Paradise" for a significant reason. Soldiers returning to the post would dismount from the streetcar as it entered the ravine and, running, they would cut across the lower parade ground and elude questioning sentries; this was significant if they had overstayed a pass.

On November 3, 1911, a regiment of soldiers at Fort Douglas prepares to move out. These soldiers may have been reassigned to another military post and are on their way to the Rio Grande Railroad station to be transported to their new post. Or they may just be going out on maneuvers. (Utah State Historical Society Photograph Collection.)

On March 7, 1911, a horse-drawn wagon is pictured in front of Fort Douglas Headquarters. The next five photographs in this chapter were taken by James William Shipler and his son Harry. The Shipler Collection of photographs is now owned by the Utah State Historical Society. James has documented life at Fort Douglas and throughout Utah since 1890, when he moved his family to Salt Lake City and opened up a photography business. (Utah State Historical Society Photograph Collection.)

This is a photograph of soldiers at Fort Douglas loading a wagon and packing equipment to be moved out on maneuvers on March 7, 1911. (Utah State Historical Society Photograph Collection.)

Soldiers are busy packing up equipment at Fort Douglas Headquarters on March 7, 1911. (Utah State Historical Society Photograph Collection.)

In 1911, sidewalks and streetlights have been installed at the fort, but the streets are still made of dirt. A solder and two female companions are taking a stroll along one of the many tree-lined street at Fort Douglas. (Utah State Historical Society Photograph Collection.)

Four

WORLD WAR I ERA

World War I began in 1914, and the country attempted to remain peaceful, but in 1917 Germany's declaration of unrestricted submarine warfare forced President Wilson to declare war. The fort had been in caretaker status for four years while the United States was having trouble along the Mexican border, but in May 1917 the 20th Infantry returned to the fort, and in a few weeks the fort was bustling with new construction and new troops. The fort became a mobilization and training post for three infantry regiments and the 145th Field Artillery, Utah National Guard. In the summer, there were 7,000 men in training—the largest number ever assigned to the post. General Hospital No. 27 was activated with beds for 1,000 casualties.

Fort Douglas became an important military facility during World War I. Recruits by the thousands were trained here. A prisoner-of-war camp was erected on the post with 870 German prisoners. Some were enemy aliens living in the United States who had pro-German sentiments. But most were navy men whose ships had been captured by American forces in Guam and Hawaii. The war ended on November 11, 1918, and the hospital was closed after handling more than 500 patients. The prison barracks finally closed in 1920.

In June 1922, Fort Douglas became the home of the 38th Infantry, the famous "Rock of the Marne" regiment. During the war, the regiment had distinguished itself when it assisted in blocking an offensive by nine German regiments and 88 batteries of field artillery in the Marne Valley.

Construction during the years before World War II included new officers' and non-commissioned officers' quarters, a golf course and polo field, a theater in 1932, and a swimming pool and bathhouse in 1937. In 1939, the large 250-man barracks and a smaller barracks for hospital personnel were completed. The 38th Infantry marched off to San Antonio, Texas, in August 1940, heading for Fort Sam Houston, ending the longest tenure by any unit at the fort.

A World War I recruitment poster in 1917 asks local civilians from Utah to sign up and be honored and respected by all.

This is a postcard entitled "R.O.T.C. Camp, Fort Douglas, Utah." The Reserve Officers' Training Corps (ROTC) concept was established in 1862 with the Morrill Act. Part of the federal government's requirements for a land-grant college was for schools to include military tactics as part of the curriculum. Fort Douglas has been a large part of, and has participated for many years in, the University of Utah's ROTC program.

This postcard is labeled "C.M.T. Camp, Fort Douglas, Utah." The Citizen's Military Training Camps operated from 1921 to 1940, giving thousands of young men, high school and college students, training in military subjects, leadership, and citizenship. They came from different backgrounds; all were young, impressionable, and eager to learn. The officers were mostly regular army, were well educated, and used good grammar and clean language. The noncoms, often with years of service, were strict, did not stand for any monkey business, and expected the young men to be soldiers.

In July 1895, work was started by the 16th Infantry on a new reservoir in Red Butte Canyon and was completed in the fall of 1896 by the 24th Infantry. Because of the population growth of the surrounding area, a new dam was started in 1928 and completed August 11, 1930, at a cost of $369,956. This new dam had the storage capacity of 124.8 million gallons of water. Jane Price, daughter of the post commander, Col. Howard Price, turned the first spade of earth. (University of Utah, Marriott Library.)

The 20th Infantry is on maneuvers in the field, and the caption on this photograph reads, "Barbering in the Field." The 20th Infantry under the command of Col. James A. Irons arrived at Fort Douglas from Honolulu, Hawaii, in October 1911. The regiment left for El Paso, Texas, to help guard the Mexican border from the terrorist actions of Pancho Villa and his followers with 38 officers and 729 enlisted men on November 29, 1913. Colonel Irons left for Tokyo, Japan, on December 1, 1913, with Lt. Col. Frederick Perkins taking command of the 20th Infantry. (University of Utah, Marriott Library.)

With tin cup and mess kit in hand, the men of the 15th Infantry line up for mess call. This photograph was taken about 1914 at an unknown location. In March 1911, the 15th Infantry was ordered to Texas to participate in guarding the Mexican border. The regiment was welcomed home by a large crowd on their return to Fort Douglas on July 16, 1911.

The days of horse and buggy are fading, and the use of automobiles in the military is starting to take hold. The soldiers in this photograph are unloading equipment off of a much-overloaded vehicle. (Utah State Historical Society Photograph Collection.)

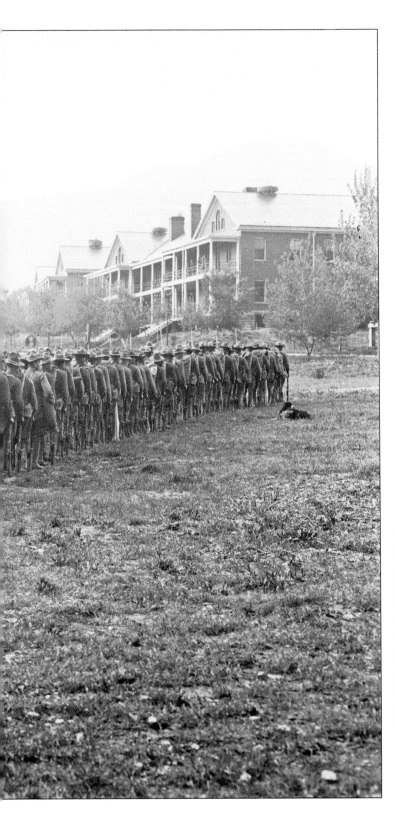

In 1917, there were approximately 4,500 new recruits and the equivalent of three regiments stationed at Fort Douglas. This influx of men brought about shortages of bedding and housing. Construction was authorized and contractors were employed to construct new barracks. Also a general hospital was established at the post in 1918. (Utah State Historical Society Photograph Collection.)

Standing at attention are some of the men of the 43rd Infantry. This photograph was taken July 27, 1917. The men were trained in hand-to-hand combat with bayonets, how to fight in trench warfare, target practice, and machine-gun training. They were instructed and prepared for combat in the European theater. (Utah State Historical Society Photograph Collection.)

On May 28, 1917, work was just about completed on the 12 buildings being constructed by James Stewart and Company for the prisoner-of-war camp that was located on the lower parade ground at Fort Douglas. Each barracks was 217 feet long and 20 feet wide and was furnished with 50 double bunk beds. (Utah State Historical Society Photograph Collection.)

The POW camp known as the Third War Prison Barracks housed about 500 German naval prisoners captured by American ships. The primary occupants were German and Austro-Hungarian aliens arrested in the western United States, totaling approximately 800. The compound would measure 922 feet by 748 feet with 12 rows of wooden cantonments that would supply the prisoners with bathhouses, sleeping quarters, mess halls, and officers' quarters. The entire compound was surrounded by two 10-foot barbed-wire fences spaced 20 feet apart. The outer fence was electrified at the top. On each corner of the fenced compound was a guard tower, each equipped with a water-cooled machine gun and searchlights. (National Archives.)

On June 10, 1917, the first 321 German naval prisoners of war arrived by train in Salt Lake City. During the early morning hours, prisoners boarded a streetcar to take them from the train station to camp. The sleeping quarters in each barracks contained 50 bunk beds for 100 men with space for a trunk. Each prisoner was furnished with a mattress, pillow, two sheets, and two blankets. (National Archives.)

The prison mess hall could serve 100 men at a time. A large woodstove was used for cooking, and the prisoners furnished their own cooks. Each mess hall was given a large icebox for keeping their food cold. (Utah State Historical Society Photograph Collection.)

Some of the prisoners with musical talent put together bands. This band is made up of German navy personnel. There was also an orchestra made up of both military and civilian prisoners that put on concerts. Col. Arthur Williams, a 68-year-old retired army officer, was called to take command of War Prison Barracks 3.

The POWs constructed a two-story YMCA building in the compound for use as a library, meeting hall, and classroom. Athletic activities were organized by the YMCA representative from Salt Lake City. A most unfortunate incident happened to Stanislaus Lewitski when he fell from the parallel bars and died later from a severed spinal column on September 13, 1917. He was buried in the Fort Douglas Cemetery with full military honors. (National Archives.)

Rev. Fred Wissenbach, POW No. 640 is the leader of the civilian prisoners' Literature Circle and is seated in the center above the sign in this image. For the most part, the POWs at Fort Douglas were treated with respect and dignity, but they were prisoners and they had to work to keep the prison operating. A group of civilian prisoners that called themselves the IWW (I Wouldn't Work) made it difficult for the camp commander and the guards to keep the atmosphere in camp at a tolerable level.

Another form of entertainment for the prisoners was the occasional play. The more serious side of the prison were the many attempts to escape that included digging tunnels, cutting through the wire fence, homemade bombs, and bribing the guards. In most cases, these attempts failed. Punishment was usually a diet of bread and water or confinement or both. In March 1920, the government closed the war prison barracks at Fort Douglas.

The 145th Field Artillery regimental football team is pictured here in 1918. They boasted of playing six games and holding their opponents scoreless. Not only did the regiments play each other, but they also played the University of Utah and other civilian teams in the surrounding area. Baseball, track and field, boxing, and polo were other sports participated in frequently at Fort Douglas.

In 1945, approximately 49 acres of federal land at the mouth of Immigration Canyon was acquired by the Utah Pioneer Trails and Landmarks Association for construction of a monument commemorating the arrival of the Mormons in the Salt Lake Valley on July 24, 1847. The monument is constructed near the spot where Brigham Young spoke the historical words, "This is the Place. Drive on." The land was granted to the association on a revocable permit.

While on a nationwide tour, Pres. Woodrow Wilson (second from the left) visited Fort Douglas on September 23, 1919. Col. George L. Byram (far left), post commander, and his wife hosted a tea in their honor. The president and his wife, Ellen Louise (third from the left), were accompanied by Gov. Simon Bamberger (fourth from the left) and his wife, Ida (third from the right), and all were greeted by a 21-gun salute. (Utah State Historical Society Photograph Collection.)

Col. Keith K. Tatom was post commander for a very short time. He also served with the Civilian Conservation Corps at Fort Douglas and had a hand in much of the fort's landscaping and needed improvements that took place in the 1930s. In 1946, he was appointed commander of the district. This photograph is labeled "29th Infantry."

In 1918, the pandemic influenza was at its peak and had already killed more people than lives lost in the Great War. Women started volunteering their time and talents in support of this world crisis. As the war ended, these wonderful women continued to do what they could to help, a tradition still going on today. Because of the flu epidemic, soldiers were ordered to remain on the train at certain stops so as not to spread or contract the flu. The ladies in this photograph are Red Cross volunteers handing out small cakes or cookies to soldiers returning home from duty in World War I.

Brig. Gen. Ulysses Grant McAlexander was post commander from January 15, 1922, to November 30, 1922. Born August 30, 1864, in Dundas, Minnesota, he graduated from West Point in 1887 and was commissioned a second lieutenant in the infantry. He served in the Spanish-American War and was on duty in the Philippines. He took command of the 38th Infantry, 3rd Infantry Division, and in July 1918 they were assigned to a portion of the Marne riverfront near Moulins, France. After holding off the German offensive, both McAlexander and the 38th Infantry were dubbed the "Rock of the Marne." He was made a brigadier general in March 1921 and retired from the military in July 1924 as a major general.

Here is a c. 1920 bugle call for the 38th Infantry. Bugles have always been an effective way to communicate over long distances and have been part of the U.S. military since the Revolutionary War. Each bugle call sends a different message: Adjutant's Call, Attention, Boots and Saddles, Call to Quarters, Charge, Church Call, Drill Call, Fatigue Call, Fire Call, Guard Mount, Mail Call, Mess Call, Officers Call, School Call, and a favorite, Payday March, which meant the soldier was going to be paid. The most recognized and emotional call used today is "Taps," which has been sounded over soldiers' graves since 1885.

Soldiers line up on the polo field. The polo field was completed, piped, and seeded in 1924 and was used for several seasons. During World War II, the area was used as a vehicle storage lot in connection with the ordnance repair shops.

Some of the loneliest times for a soldier are during the holidays; they are missing their families and the holiday traditions that go along with family life. To help keep the morale up at Fort Douglas in 1927, Company H, 38th Infantry, celebrated Christmas with a formal Christmas dinner.

Thanksgiving
1917

MACHINE GUN COMPANY, 20TH INFANTRY
FORT DOUGLAS, UTAH

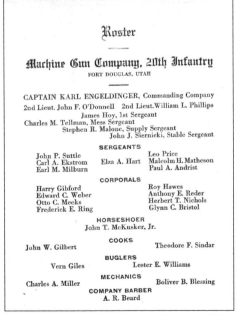

Roster

Machine Gun Company, 20th Infantry
FORT DOUGLAS, UTAH

CAPTAIN KARL ENGELDINGER, Commanding Company
2nd Lieut. John F. O'Donnell   2nd Lieut. William L. Phillips
James Hoy, 1st Sergeant
Charles M. Tellman, Mess Sergeant
Stephen R. Malone, Supply Sergeant
John J. Siernicki, Stable Sergeant

SERGEANTS

John P. Suttle   Leo Price
Carl A. Ekstrom   Elza A. Hart   Malcolm H. Matheson
Earl M. Milburn   Paul A. Andrist

CORPORALS

Harry Gibford   Roy Hawes
Edward C. Weber   Anthony E. Reder
Otto C. Meeks   Herbert T. Nichols
Frederick E. Ring   Glynn C. Bristol

HORSESHOER
John T. McKusker, Jr.

COOKS
John W. Gilbert   Theodore F. Sindar

BUGLERS
Vern Giles   Lester E. Williams

MECHANICS
Charles A. Miller   Boliver B. Blessing

COMPANY BARBER
A. R. Beard

This is the menu from Thanksgiving 1917 for Machine Gun Company, 20th Infantry, at Fort Douglas, Utah. Not only did the menu list the food being served, but it also had a company roster. It is very interesting that besides listing all the soldiers in this particular company, it also listed the company barber, horses, mules, dogs, and Dutch the company cat.

Here is a view of the squad room in one of the Fort Douglas barracks on December 8, 1928. This barracks was used by Company I, 38th Infantry. The barracks have not changed much since the 1800s; a soldier was issued a pillow, two blankets, sheets, a footlocker for personal items, and a locker to hang his uniform. (Utah State Historical Society.)

This is actually a postcard of soldiers marching on Soldier's Circle. Between 1904 and 1910, more barracks were constructed on what is known as Soldier's Circle—six barracks to house 176 men plus a smaller barracks for the band that housed 33 men. These buildings were made of red brick rather than the sandstone used on earlier barracks and buildings. They are still in use today by the reserves.

Col. Howard C. Price was the commander at Fort Douglas from August 1928 through December 1931. One of the more important improvements to the fort during his command was the construction of a new dam in Red Butte Canyon. In 1930, he helped organize a program of training called the Citizens' Military Training Camps (CMTC). In a talk before the Salt Lake City Service Club, Colonel Price said, "Fort Douglas is a compact little town of 1,050 with its own hospital, library, theater, bowling alley, gymnasium, service club, and stores. It is a complete unit, with its own telephone system, fire department, and police system, including a jail."

At the height of the Depression, President Roosevelt signed a bill creating the Civilian Conservation Corps (CCC), and in weeks construction started on several Utah camps. The CCC aimed to provide work for the nation's estimated 5 to 7 million unemployed young men who ranged in age from 16 to 25. The Fort Douglas CCC District was started in May 1933 with headquarters at Fort Douglas. CCC monthly wages ranged from $30 to $45, with $22 of that allotted to dependants or deposited with the government until their discharge. They were given food, clothing, medical care, an education, and the opportunity to learn a trade plus the adventure of working in the great outdoors.

By 1938, there were over 6,000 enrollees in 38 camps in the Fort Douglas CCC District with 100 commissioned officers in command. With the help of these officers, thousands of young men left the CCC and went into useful and profitable jobs. Not only did the men profit but also the country profited from their work. Most of the Fort Douglas District jobs consisted of forestry work, firefighting, the improvement of grazing land, soil conservation, national and state park work, and policing.

Motorcycles started showing up in the military in the early part of the 20th century. Light and maneuverable, they started replacing horses as mounts for scouts and messengers, and they were widely used by the military police and others with similar duties. They could travel without roads and had minimal requirements for fuel and maintenance.

Maj. Gen. Walter C. Sweeney served as Fort Douglas commander from April 4, 1935, to December 15, 1936.

One of the more celebrated conductors to lead a Fort Douglas Band was the famous 38th Infantry's Chief Warrant Officer Leopold Antone Yost. After World War I, American forces commander Gen. John J. Pershing praised Yost for directing "the best band overseas." Chief Yost died in 1951 and is buried in the post cemetery.

In the summer of 1940, the 38th Infantry Band moved to Texas. A farewell concert was held with Warrant Officer Yost leading his band. The 38th remained at Fort Douglas until 1940, and many Salt Lake residents remember the post band concerts and the military reviews and parades with great nostalgia.

Officers and enlisted men at Fort Douglas took turns hosting dances. The side of this wagon from the 1930s is advertising a "Red Butte Dance, Friday Night." Young women from Salt Lake City attended the dance, and the 38th Infantry Band supplied the music.

Officers from the 38th Infantry stand in front of Building 32, regimental headquarters, at Fort Douglas. After only six weeks of training, the 38th Infantry landed in France on April 14, 1918. On May 30, they were rushed to the neighborhood of Chateau-Thierry to support the French in holding the Chateau-Thierry Bridge. By July 15, there were men in every company who had either killed Germans or who had fired at them at close range.

July 15, 1918, brought a continuous succession of arriving shells down on the 38th Infantry in France until 7:55 a.m., and then the moderately heavy schedule began, including tear and sneezing gas shells on forward areas and lethal gas on supports and reserves. This is a soldier from the 38th Infantry with a .30-caliber water-cooled machine gun.

By 12:15 p.m. on July 16, 1918, at the Chateau-Thierry Bridge, every man in the regiment had adjusted his gas mask to wear for the next six or seven hours and had reached his previously constructed splinter-proof slit trench. The bombardment on the front lines was intense until 3:30 a.m., when the beginning of the rolling barrage and attack started. Through the fog, mist, and smoke, one could see boats being filled and pioneer troops hauling pontoons into place. Men from the 38th Infantry at Fort Douglas pose with their .30-caliber water-cooled machine gun.

After holding off the German advance in critical areas along the front, the 38th Infantry was given the name "Rock of the Marne." General Pershing, in his final report, stated, "On this occasion a single regiment of the Third Division wrote one of the most brilliant pages of our military annals. It prevented the crossing on certain points of its front, while on either flank the Germans, who had gained a footing, pressed forward. Our men, firing in three directions, met the German attacks with counter-attacks at critical points and succeeded in throwing two German Divisions into complete confusion, capturing 600 prisoners." These men from the 38th Infantry stand at attention in front of the Fort Douglas fire station.

The commander's quarters, Building 620, was constructed in 1875 and was once a barracks for 40 men. It was remodeled in 1912 and used for administrative offices. Then in 1929, it was again remodeled and used to house the post commander. (National Archives.)

This is the interior of Building 620 around 1930. (National Archives.)

The commander's quarters building has been restored by the University of Utah and is used today for meetings and receptions. The beautiful wood floors and fireplace are back, and the wood ceiling and dark wood beams have also been restored. (National Archives.)

The original bandstand was destroyed by fire in 1910, and this new structure was built on the same spot. Made of concrete and iron, this bandstand was not quite as elegant as the first one, but for sure it was not going to catch fire. The Rock of the Marne Band used this structure until they were transferred to Texas in 1940.

Gov. George H. Dern is shown with Col. Howard C. Price reviewing the 38th Infantry at Fort Douglas. Dern was governor of Utah from 1925 to 1933. He was a successful businessman, mining man, politician, and a friend to the military. Later he became the Secretary of War, a position he held until his death in 1936. (Utah State Historical Society Photograph Collection.)

During the Depression years of the 1930s, the principal improvements to the post consisted of installation of walks, curbing, new roads, and landscaping improvements such as the building of retaining walls and an extensive tree and shrub planting program. The work was done with Works Progress Administration (WPA) labor and the Civilian Conservation Corps program. These men are working on Potter Street at Fort Douglas.

Roadwork is taking place on Soldier's Circle at Fort Douglas. The WPA was part of Pres. Franklin D. Roosevelt's New Deal in 1933. This program put 8.5 million jobless people to work with Uncle Sam meeting the payroll. Roosevelt favored unemployment programs based on work relief rather than welfare.

Men are at work on a new road at the Post Exchange Service Station. Under the WPA, buildings, roads, schools, and even airports were constructed. The National Youth Administration gave part-time employment to students, established training programs, and provided aid to unemployed youth.

The War Department Theater was built of red brick and was completed in 1932, with a seating capacity of 398. The cost for this building was $20,000. The theater is still used today by the reserves who reside at Fort Douglas. (Utah State Historical Society Photograph Collection.)

Five

WORLD WAR II ERA

Fort Douglas became an Army Air Base in 1940 when the 7th Bombardment Group arrived. Flying training was carried on at Salt Lake Air Base, located on the municipal airport. The 7th Bomb Group departed Fort Douglas in November 1941, destination Hawaii. They arrived on December 7, right in the middle of the Japanese sneak attack on Pearl Harbor and the army airfields. The two flights of B-17s landed at various airfields on Oahu, but one landed on a golf course and another landed with its tail burning. One man was killed.

After the Pearl Harbor attack, there were fears of Japanese attacks on West Coast installations, and in January 1942 the 9th Service Command Headquarters was moved from the Presidio, San Francisco, to Fort Douglas. The command handled all supply, maintenance, hospitals, military police, and non-combat training for a nine-state area. A new building, now the University Annex, was constructed to accommodate the new personnel. The post was expanded to include a Reception and Induction Center, a Separation Center, an enlarged hospital, and an Army Finance Center. Another prisoner-of-war camp was established at Fort Douglas in the spring of 1945, and approximately 250 Italian POWs were interned behind barbed wire in a group of old Civilian Conservation Corps buildings on the lower post. The fort directed the repair and salvage of military vehicles, managed several army schools, and housed three military police companies. The MPs were used to patrol downtown Salt Lake City and Ogden and to ride the passenger trains between the West Coast and Chicago.

A group of WACs (Women's Army Corps) was assigned to the post in 1943. Several female officers supplemented the headquarters staff, and in April 1944 two enlisted WACs were assigned to 9th Service Command public relations offices. No other enlisted women were stationed at the post during the war.

In August 1944, the post was invaded by 220 WAVES (Women Accepted for Voluntary Emergency Services), assigned to Clearfield Naval Supply Depot but without quarters. While their quarters were being built, the women occupied some dormitory buildings at Fort Douglas.

The Ninth Service Command was disbanded in 1946, and its functions returned to the Presidio, San Francisco.

The 38th Infantry Dance Band, or Rock of the Marne Band as it was sometimes known, was led by S.Sgt. Leo B. Leonard. Leo fell in love with the lead singer, seated to the left of him, and later married her. The band was in great demand during the 1930s and played for many events at the Coconut Grove, the largest ballroom in the United States at the time, later known as the Terrace Ballroom, located at 464 South Main Street in downtown Salt Lake City.

At the outbreak of World War II, Fort Douglas assumed a position of prominence when the War Department decided to move the Ninth Corps Area Headquarters inland from San Francisco for security reasons on January 3, 1942. Sgt. William G. Ryan, motor sergeant, and PFC Donald T. Drockman are checking motor vehicles in the post motor pool at Fort Douglas in 1942. (National Archives.)

While on a fund drive for savings bonds in 1942, Bud Abbott and Lou Costello visited Fort Douglas. They had a live radio broadcast outside on the field in Soldier's Circle on KDYL Radio. This was a photo opportunity for the media with Abbot and Costello being hauled off by the MPs. (National Archives.)

This is the Fort Douglas post library as pictured in 1942. By 1942, Fort Douglas was its own little city. One could find on post a library, bowling alley, Post Exchange, swimming pool, golf course, baseball diamond, hospital, recreation center, and gas station. (National Archives.)

At one of Utah's ski resorts, Pvt. Julian McLandor, in this ski uniform, from Company B, 503rd Parachute Battalion, is taking a break with the company mascot, Goldie, on January 29, 1942. Utah is known for its great snow, and many men from para-ski troops were trained here. Some of the trainees had never seen snow until they arrived at Fort Douglas for their training period, but by the time their training was concluded, they were considered expert skiers. (U.S. Army Signal Corps.)

Fort Douglas had its own ski shop to equip the para-ski troops training at the post. These two workmen are at various stages of assembling the old wooden skis on December 26, 1943. (National Archives.)

Boxing attracted more attention and interest at Fort Douglas than any other sport. Each company had its own boxing team, which competed with other company teams for the post boxing championship. In addition to team bouts, a series of contests were held each spring to determine the post individual championships in each weight. (National Archives.)

One of many famous boxers, Jack Dempsey is seen here shaking hands with soldiers while visiting the reception center at Fort Douglas in 1942. (National Archives.)

Another famous boxer, Henry Armstrong visited the reception center at Fort Douglas in 1943. Armstrong went a few rounds with soldiers, giving tips on the fine points of boxing. (National Archives.)

Teletype operators Muriel Erickson (left) and Josephine Clay show off the new 24-hour clock built by the Signal Corps Photo Lab, 9th Service Command. (National Archives.)

Movie stars entertained the troops at the Fort Douglas Reception Center with a skit called "In the Army Now" in 1942. The honorary cook is Ralph Bellemy with M.Sgt. Jean Parker, and on KP is Allen Jenkins. (National Archives.)

Soldiers serving in the mess hall at Fort Douglas are S.Sgt. Gordon Wilson (far right) as acting mess sergeant with cooks 5th Grade Tech Cpl. John C. Hitchcock (far left), 4th Grade Tech Sgt. Reynold W. Brundage (second from the left), and 5th Grade Tech Cpl. Marion Donovin (second from the right) in 1942. (National Archives.)

Although no ground force training units were stationed at Fort Douglas during World War II, the military population was close to 1,000 officers and enlisted men at the peak of activity in the fall of 1943, with twice that many civilians. As more and more military personnel were released for overseas service, the military population declined sharply and the civilian total rose. In the basement of one of the Fort Douglas buildings, civilian personnel are working on typewriters in the Machine Records Unit.

The reception center at Fort Douglas was organized in December 1940 in a little tent village, which had formerly housed summer groups of CMTC trainees. New frame buildings were completed in 1941 on the lower post, and the center was expanded. (National Archives.)

By February 1941, the reception center was in full operation and busy receiving new recruits with the objective of classifying and assigning the newcomers to the military from a three-state area. On March 23, 1942, new recruits are arriving at the reception center. (National Archives.)

New recruits receive a lecture on the benefits of government life insurance at the Fort Douglas Reception Center on March 14, 1942. (National Archives.)

One of the most important tests given at the reception center was the Army General Classification Test (AGCT). This aptitude test would help classify or place the new soldier in an area of the military that best suited his abilities. There were 150 multiple-choice questions, and they had 40 minutes to take the test. High scores could get one into a prime position in Officer Candidate School or the Army Air Forces. (National Archives.)

The 15-minute interview with the classification specialist counted as much toward where a soldier would be placed as the AGCT. The specialist noted education, work experience, and training, even sports played and hobbies. Gen. Lewis Hershey liked to say, "I haven't seen a draft questionnaire yet in which the guy said he shot people for a living." (National Archives.)

Selectees await the classification interview in the private booths at the reception center at Fort Douglas. There were many misplacements of inductees at these centers because of the hundreds of recruits who were marched through these facilities on a weekly basis. Mistakes included the banker who became a baker because of a typing error. (National Archives.)

The physical examination was the most important part of the process and was conducted in assembly-line style with 25 men passing through every hour. The inductees went through one end and came out the other with a number around their necks or on the backs of their hands that indicated accepted or rejected. (National Archives.)

A new recruit receives an X-ray at the Fort Douglas Reception Center on March 16, 1942. Every recruit was given an X-ray to make sure he was able to do strenuous training and able to fight in combat. (National Archives.)

As part of their processing, the new inductees were vaccinated and inoculated for many of the common diseases. The first series of shots given at the reception center were usually smallpox and typhoid and were often called the "hook." The shots were never given, though, until after the inductee had been processed through the Army General Classification Test. (National Archives.)

Selectees receive their oath of office at the reception center on March 18, 1942. If the inductee passed his interview, tests, and physical, he would then sign his induction papers and be given a serial number to memorize. Inductees were assembled, an officer spoke to the men for a few moments, they were asked to raise their right hand, and the oath was administered. (National Archives.)

One of the first stops at the reception center was to receive an issue of clothing. Because there was a shortage of uniforms in the early years, many inductees were issued secondhand uniforms and others were issued uniforms from World War I. There were no real standard sizes, so if a man put on a uniform and could button it up it was loose enough, and if he could stand without it falling off it was a perfect fit. Shoes were issued with greater care. Sometimes they used an X-ray device called a fluoroscope to make sure they fit right. Some inductees were asked to carry a bucketful of sand in each hand while wearing the shoes to represent the weight of a pack that he would be carrying. (National Archives.)

Part of military training at the reception center included how to salute, military courtesy, and close order drills. AWOL and desertion articles were lectured on. An army tradition is the reading of the Articles of War, which dates back to the Continental Army and is also known as the army's criminal code. (National Archives.)

Mess officers at the reception center were under the command of Col. Harold P. Kayser in 1942. Maj. Albert B. Woolums, executive officer, watches Capt. Reed N. Colvin, the mess officer, inspect and serve homemade ice cream in the mess hall. (National Archives.)

Pvt. Gerald Ryan of Headquarters, 9th Corps Area, reflects the attitude of the average American soldier when he is served ice cream for dessert. (National Archives.)

On March 18, 1942, the reception center's Visitor Lounge at Fort Douglas is full of wives, children, mothers, and fathers of inductees waiting to see and visit with their loved ones. (National Archives.)

This is a view of the Post Exchange (PX) at Fort Douglas on March 17, 1942. The PX is an important part of a military post. It is a place to relax, get together with friends, and enjoy extra comforts, a distraction from the strict discipline of military life. (National Archives.)

While on a visit to the Fort Douglas Hospital, Mickey Rooney spends a few moments in the day room entertaining hospital patients and staff with Wally Williams, a patient at the hospital. He also visited the various rooms and brought smiles to patients confined to their beds. (National Archives.)

A Fort Douglas Hospital patient takes interest in articles that were made by other hospital patients at the dedication of the Red Cross auditorium on December 11, 1943. (National Archives.)

The Connor Bowl, named after Gen. Patrick Connor, is shown at Fort Douglas on June 3, 1943. The 9th Service Command Headquarters put together a band in July 1943, which eventually became the 364th Army Service Forces Band. They played numerous engagements in the Connor Bowl, the theater, on the parade ground, and at many public functions and parades. A regular weekly radio program was arranged, and the program was broadcast from a special studio in the band barracks.

The MP Color Guard appeared each night at the Days of '47 rodeo in Salt Lake City, July 20 through July 24, 1943, as part of the patriotic pageant. The color bearer is Sgt. Edgar J. Dunnigan, and the guards are Pvt. James E. Kelly (left) and Pvt. Rudolph Lipovsek (right). All are part of the SCU 1902 MPs. This photograph appeared in the post newspaper, the *Vedette*, on August 5, 1943, on page 7.

The Fort Douglas football team of 1944 is on Stilwell Field. Football and baseball were both well-attended sports by the soldiers and citizens of Salt Lake City. During the war, Fort Douglas produced baseball and softball teams, which made good showings in the surrounding communities. Each company had a team, and each team played against other companies, universities, and civilian teams from Salt Lake City. (U.S. Army Signal Corps.)

In 1944, troops from Fort Douglas march down Main Street in Salt Lake City, past the Mormon Temple and Brigham Young monument, to inaugurate the May Drive for War Bonds in Utah. (National Archives.)

Everyone was affected by the war; every household in America had to pull together to help win the war and bring loved ones home. An article in the *Roosevelt Standard* on January 2, 1942, read, "We must begin to produce and conserve far out of proportion to our own requirements . . . we will do all this cheerfully and freely, secure in the belief that America is great enough and right enough to win what her people will." The photograph is of Beth Mortensen at home with her brother Rex.

Civilians working for the War Department at Fort Douglas in 1942 are buying war bonds. Upon entry into World War II by the United States, savings bonds became known as war bonds, a way to raise money for the war. They were also known as war loans or victory bonds, and the first Series E was sold to Pres. Franklin D. Roosevelt on May 1, 1941. (National Archives.)

The Post Exchange has changed a lot since the beginning of World War II when it was used mostly as a social center. The PX in this photograph taken in 1954 does not have the counter that served coffee and donuts but more of a family-oriented department store atmosphere. (National Archives.)

The Fort Douglas fire station in 1955 includes the fire chief's pickup truck parked out front along with a Class 75 truck and Class 325 Dodge. This wood-framed building was constructed in 1942 and is in use today as a storage and exhibit preparation shop for the Fort Douglas Museum.

The 38th Infantry Rock of the Marne Monument was dedicated in October 1965. The bronze plaque bears the regimental shield with its broken chevron, representing the break in the German attack, a rock signifying the regiment's title, and below this shield the words "Rock of the Marne." The whole has for its basis the 3rd Division insignia. This monument is located at the east end of Stilwell Field.

In the 6th U.S. Army 1957 Mountain Division Preliminary Golf Tournament, the Senior Division members from left to right are Col. H. E. Brooks, M.Sgt. Kenneth K. Evans, SPC G. A. Waite, M.Sgt. C. Ackley, and LTC E. M. Robertson. At the instruction of Brig. Gen. U. G. McAlexander, commanding officer of the post in the early 1920s, the present golf course was laid out. Local sportsmen interested in developing the project formed the Fort Douglas Golf Club, which put up the money for the materials, and General McAlexander furnished the labor. The civilian club was limited in membership, but army personnel were to have free use of the facilities since the course was entirely within the reservation at the time.

Receptions, reviews, change-of-commands, dining in, and dining out were all part of military life at the fort and most were formal in nature. From left to right, Mrs. P. M. Rifleman, Mrs. J. D. Rifleman, and Mrs. John U. Schiess are being served refreshments at a reception in honor of Col. H. E. Brooks, chief, Utah Military Division, at the Fort Douglas Officers' Club.

Six

CLOSING THE FORT

During the many years since the end of World War II, the army submitted proposals to close the post because it was too small with nowhere to grow; Salt Lake City and the University of Utah had expanded to encompass the fort. In 1967, they officially lowered the flag and placed the post under Fort Carson, Colorado, as a sub-post. Fort Douglas continued as a support post for army, navy, and marine reserves and Utah National Guard. The post did operate as an Induction and Separation Center during the Korean and Vietnam Wars.

The University of Utah was granted 60 acres of land in 1894, and a number of additional grants have been given over the years. By 1947, office, warehouse, and storage space that exceeded the army's needs was parceled out to various federal agencies.

War Assets Administration, charged with disposing of millions of dollars worth of surplus war material in the area, leased the entire Separation Center area, including more than 20 buildings on the lower post. Other buildings were turned over to the Bureau of Mines and Public Buildings Administration.

Fort Douglas was closed on October 26, 1991. The University of Utah received all but 64 acres, which the Stephen A. Douglas Armed Forces Reserve Center retained. Sen. Jake Garn of Utah attached an amendment to the Military Construction Bill for 1991, transferring the fort to the University of Utah. President Bush signed the bill on November 5, and it specified, "The conveyance may be made only on condition that—The state of Utah agrees to maintain and operate the Army museum located on the land. . . . The University of Utah agrees to maintain and operate the Army chapel and other historical buildings located on the land, . . . and to preserve and maintain the parade grounds."

In 1999, the university again received 11 acres for student housing that was also used for the 2002 Winter Olympic Village.

The Separation Center was established November 7, 1944, and during the demobilization period, it was the last stopover on the road home for thousands of joyous GIs who received their discharges there. The last man was discharged on July 12, 1947, when the closing of the center was ordered by the War Department. The total number of men separated up to that time was 53,617, not including 7,317 officers processed for relief from active duty.

Utah National Guard headquarters was established in Building 97, adjacent to post headquarters. The National Guard received a total of 33 buildings, including pistol, rifle, skeet, anti-aircraft, machine-gun, and shotgun ranges and a gas chamber. (Utah National Guard.)

When the reception center was closed in September 1946, only the induction station remained of what had once been the busiest section of the post, the War Department Personnel Center. A brief increase in activity resulted in October 1946, when Fort Douglas was directed to reopen its separation facility to process personnel in the vicinity who were eligible for release, rather than sending them to the two main centers at Camp Beale, California, and Fort Lewis, Washington. Pictured here is the Memorial Day Service on May 30, 1944, on Stilwell Field. (Photograph by Signal Corps, U.S. Army.)

The Veterans Administration received the southwest corner of the reservation for a 500-bed hospital by a Congress-approved land grant. The Shriners' Hospital obtained land for a building site near the old gravel pit on the north side of the reservation by an act of Congress on March 14, 1946. The organization paid $8,500 for the land. This is Fort Douglas (center) as it looked in the 1960s, with the Veterans Hospital in the lower right corner.

The University of Utah and its Naval and Army ROTC units leased the former headquarters annex, Building 105, for classrooms, took over the WAC barracks for dormitories, acquired the tent camp area for training, the athletic fields for recreation, and additional buildings for storage. In all, the university property included 61 of the post's buildings and the golf course. This is Building 108 on Soldier's Circle.

Following World War II, the GI Bill of Rights was passed, giving money for tuition, books, and other expenses to war veterans so they could attend school. There was a rapid growth in attendance of colleges and universities in Utah. The enrollment doubled at the University of Utah and the students and their families needed a place to live, so A. Ray Olpin, the president of the university, eased the overcrowding on campus by filling some of the facilities at Fort Douglas.

Through the efforts of Maj. Gen. Michael B. Kauffman, a museum was established in 1976 inside one of the old stone barracks. Today the museum is administered by the Utah National Guard and supported by the Fort Douglas Museum Association.

BIBLIOGRAPHY

Arrington, Leonard J., and Thomas G. Alexander. "The U.S. Army Overlooks Salt Lake Valley, Fort Douglas, 1862–1965." *Utah Historical Quarterly*. Fall 1965: vol. 33, No. 4.

Cunningham, Raymond K. Jr. *Prisoners at Fort Douglas, War Prison Barracks Three and the Enemy Aliens, 1917–1920*. Salt Lake City: Fort Douglas Military Museum, 1983.

Evans, John Henry. *Story of Utah*. New York: Macmillan Publishers, 1933.

Hibbard, Charles G. *Fort Douglas, Utah: A Frontier Fort 1862–1991*. Fort Collins, CO: Vestige Press Publishing Company, 1999.

James, G. W. *Utah, Land of Blossoming Valleys*. Boston: The Page Company, 1922.

Kennett, Lee. *The American Soldier in World War II*. Norman, OK: University of Oklahoma Press, 1997.

Littig, Capt. Melvin J. *The Battle of Bear River*. 1977.

McCarthy, M. R. *Patrick Edward Connor, A Closer Look*. Salt Lake City: Fort Douglas Military Museum, 1983.

Neff, Andrew L. *History of Utah, 1847–1869*. Salt Lake City: Deseret New Press, 1940.

Pedersen, Lyman C. Jr. "The Daily Union Vedette: A Military Voice on the Mormon Frontier." *Utah Historical Quarterly*. Vol. 42.

Rogers, Fred B. *Soldiers of the Overland*. San Francisco: Grabhorn Press, 1938.

Stegner, Wallace. *Mormon Country*. New York: Duell, Sloan and Pearce, 1942.

Tate, Michael L. *The Frontier Army in the Settlement of the West, The Union Vedette*. 1942, 1943, 1944, and 1945.

University of Utah. *Historic Fort Douglas at the University of Utah, A Brief History & Walking Tour*. 2000.

Utley, Robert M. *Frontiersmen in Blue: the United States Army and the Indian, 1848–1865*. New York: Macmillan Publishers, 1967.

DISCOVER THOUSANDS OF LOCAL HISTORY BOOKS FEATURING MILLIONS OF VINTAGE IMAGES

Arcadia Publishing, the leading local history publisher in the United States, is committed to making history accessible and meaningful through publishing books that celebrate and preserve the heritage of America's people and places.

Find more books like this at
www.arcadiapublishing.com

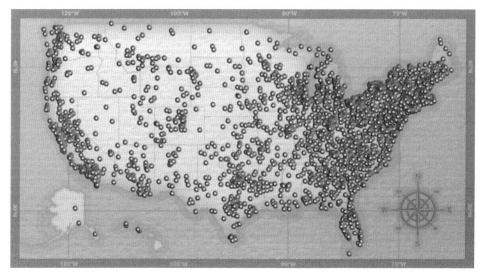

Search for your hometown history, your old stomping grounds, and even your favorite sports team.

Consistent with our mission to preserve history on a local level, this book was printed in South Carolina on American-made paper and manufactured entirely in the United States. Products carrying the accredited Forest Stewardship Council (FSC) label are printed on 100 percent FSC-certified paper.

MADE IN THE USA